Generalized Anxiety Disorder Relief:

Simple And Easily Adoptable Self Help Guide To Relieve Generalized Anxiety Disorder Naturally

By Joshua Sideon

Table of Contents

Introduction

Congratulations on purchasing *Generalized Anxiety Disorder Relief: Simple And Easily Adoptable Self Help Guide To Relieve Generalized Anxiety Disorder Naturally*. If you have purchased this book, then it means you are curious about the signs, symptoms, and changed lifestyle that revolves around General Anxiety Disorder. Maybe you are not sure if you have it, or maybe you have been recently diagnosed and are looking for materials on how to cope with this newfound direction your life has taken. If you want to be educated on the signs, statistics, symptoms, and natural ways to relieve general anxiety from your life, then you have come to the right place.

First of all, understand that you are not alone. Over 6 million adults residing in the U.S. are currently diagnosed with G.A.D., and it is usually categorized by a persistent and excessive worry of the things and life surrounding you. A number of different things can trigger G.A.D. episodes, and for some the mere idea of getting through the day can be overwhelming enough to trigger specific reclusive and worrisome episodes. People who have to find ways to deal with G.A.D. find it very difficult, and sometimes impossible, to control their worries, and they might worry more than appropriate over things that actually do require their worry.

People who struggle with this disorder experience increasing amounts of anxiety brought on by their worry, and sometimes someone can find themselves worrying about a "worst case scenario," even though there has been no substantiated evidence brought to the table that states that type of worry is necessary. Individuals who struggle with this disorder also anticipate disaster more than others and usually find themselves overly concerned and controlling over things such as money, work, and familial dramas.

G.A.D. is usually officially diagnosed when it has been proven, via pre-established doctoral visits, that the worry they experience is not only frequent, but hard to control. Once a pattern is established with a doctor, a diagnosis is given and medicinal interventions are usually attempted.

However, medicine is not always required to help relieve excessive worry and anxiety.

Within the walls of this text you will find various statistics to help paint the picture that you are not alone as well as multiple natural remedies you can implement in order to help abate your anxiety and worries. Contrary to popular belief, anxiety can be cured when these types of interventions are taken on for the long haul, and can actually result in those previously diagnosed with G.A.D. coming off medication and frequent doctor's visits altogether.

The answers found within this book will not only enable you to live a life that is free from the shackles of your worry and anxiety, these answers will also help you to pinpoint whether you have anxiety and worrisome symptoms that should be looked at by a doctor. That is an important distinction, however: this book does not condone the use of these practices without first consulting a physician. There are many other underlying causes that need to be considered and tested for before a G.A.D. diagnosis is given, and your physician should always be updated on tactics you are utilizing in order to abate and control your worries and anxieties.

The information found within this book will not only help you to find alternative ways to treat your anxiety, it will also help you to figure out whether you need to see a doctor for worries and anxieties you already experience. This book is not simply for those who have already been diagnosed… it is also for those who feel there is something innately wrong with their anxieties and worries, but are still unwilling to schedule a visit with a doctor.

I can promise you this book will not only give you a piece of mind, it will also give you a piece of your life back. Whether it is in the form of clarity and gaining the confidence to contact your doctor, or whether it is in the form of ditching those dozens of orange pill bottles for something more substantial and self-sustaining, this book will help you navigate those areas of your life in order to provide you the answers you seek.

Please, if you have not yet purchased this book, I urge you to. This book is not simply full of self-help suggestions, this book is full of statistics and researched information that can help shed light on a darkened journey you have been traveling.

Do not wait. Turn on that flashlight and start looking around you. G.A.D., and the issues that surround it, can be difficult to cope with and even harder to admit if you do not have an official diagnosis. If going to the doctor makes you feel anxious, then understand that seeing your physician for this anxiousness is no different than seeing them when you have a sinus infection or the flu. The mind is just as important as the body, and physicians treat all aspects of the body, not just the physical. They are not there to label you, they are there to help you. Your anxiety is producing physical symptoms that should be evaluated, and there is nothing wrong with that.

Not only will this book show you that you are not alone, it will also show you how to manage it on your own, no matter the medications anyone might attempt to shove in your direction.

Chapter One
What G.A.D. Entails

This book is going to provide for you simple and practical tips in order to drastically reduce the anxiety with which you battle. The overwhelming sensations that overcome the body when anxieties and worries begin to take over can make it seem as if you are drowning in an ocean when all you are doing is sipping on a glass of water, and it can make it hard to get through a simple day. And, for some, the mere idea of getting through a day is hazardous enough.

However, there are many things that need to be addressed in order to pinpoint whether G.A.D. is something you should be worried about or whether there is another underlying cause for what you are feeling and going through.

The potential causes of G.A.D. are:

- A family history of anxiety.

- A family history of other gene-based or psychological-based disorders.

- Recent (or prolonged) exposure to a traumatic or stressful event, such as a family-related debacle or even a physical ailment or illness.

- Childhood abuse.

- The excessive utilization of alcohol and/or tobacco, as these can exacerbate symptoms of anxiety.

- Recent, and traumatic, abuse.

- PTSD.

- Abandonment (or feelings thereof).

- Suffering of a major loss, such as a death in the family or of a close friend.

While this is a comprehensive list of the most common causes and triggers of G.A.D., this list does not summarize the whole of the web of things that could cause this type of anxiety-based disorder to trigger. If you do not spot any one of your triggers on this list, that does not ultimately mean you are not suffering with General Anxiety Disorder. So, let's take a look at the list of symptoms that come with these episodes:

Symptoms of G.A.D. include:

- Difficulty sleeping.

- Difficulty concentrating.

- Fatigue and/or exhaustion.

- Uncontrollable irritability.

- Repeated stomach aches and/or sessions of diarrhea.

- Muscle tension.

- Sweaty palms.

- Shaking.

- A rapid heartbeat.

- Tingling or numbness within different parts of the body.

- Perspiration of the forehead or back of the neck.

- Tunnel vision.

- Dry mouth.

- Restlessness.

- An unrealistic view of problems.

- Trouble staying asleep.

- Being easily startled.

Again, this list of symptoms, while comprehensive, do not begin to consider the whole of the symptoms out there that are experienced by individuals who deal with attacks of worry, panic, and anxiety. This list is simply a compilation of the most common symptoms individuals experience and symptoms doctors have witnessed with their own eyes.

But, maybe you have purchased this guide because you are not sure as to whether you are experiencing sessions of excessive worry or anxiety. Maybe you are looking for someone to tell you exactly what happens when these attacks occur. Well, if that is what you are looking for, then you have come to the right place.

When someone experiences as G.A.D. attack, it usually involves:

- A surge of overwhelming panic.

- Feeling of losing control (or going crazy).

- A feeling akin to passing out.

- A rapidly surging heart rate.

- Hyperventilation.

- Shaking and/or trembling.

- Involuntary tears.

A feeling of detachment, or feeling as if they world around you is not real.

- An overwhelming sense of fear.

- Hot and/or cold flashes.

- Nausea or cramping of the stomach.

- An inability to control the thoughts of your mind.

It is important to always keep in mind that this comprehensive list is of the most common symptoms and episodes experienced during a G.A.D. attack. It does not even begin to comprise a list of all the symptoms to date that are experienced by someone having these attacks. And it can be a very scary thing, especially if you do not understand what is happening. But, G.A.D. is not just limited to adults, it can also occur in children, especially if the issue is brain chemistry-based. Several studies have shown us that there are certain genes in a human's DNA that make someone more prone to developing this type of disorder and all of its offshoots (such as PTSD and other panic disorders), which means that children are prone to this as well.

If you are worried about your child, then there are some things to look out for that could potentially signal to you that your child is on the verge of developing G.A.D.:

- Perfectionism, which usually comes with excessive self-criticism and an irrational fear of making mistakes.

- Identifying with the "belief" that misfortune is contagious and that it will eventually happen to them anyway.

- The overarching feeling that any life disaster experienced is their fault and that they were somehow the reason for everything "falling apart" (like the mental train-of-thought that comes with children of divorce).

- The constant need for frequent amounts of reassurance and approval in order to feel rooted in their own self-confidence.

If your child is displaying any of these symptoms, then it is worth talking to a doctor about. The quicker you can diagnose it, the quicker you can help your child cope with it.

But, that standard is not simply for children. If you are an adult and you are experiencing anything listed above, then the quicker you get it checked out and diagnosed, the quicker you can help yourself when it comes to coping with this reality.

There are many things that people who struggle with G.A.D. need, but the biggest one is support. Social interaction with someone who truly cares for you when you are going through this is going to be one of the greatest reinforcers of strength, courage, and personal perseverance you can obtain. Likewise, you need to be able to establish someone you can go and talk to about these types of issues and episodes without being told you are "lesser than" or "a burden"... because you are not.

Therefore, it is imperative that someone struggling with G.A.D. get rid of any unhealthy relationships that surround them. Unhealthy relationships and the patterns they establish will do nothing but spiral you into worlds of unnecessary worry and anxiety over the insecurities you have with the relationship. Ask yourself these questions: does the person you have this relationship with withdraw at random times and starve you of their presence? Do they intentionally test you? Do they make broad accusations to bring you down or saddle you with some sort of unidentifiable blame? Are they unnecessarily clingy? If any of these are present in relationships you have with others, it is worth considering what type of positive atmosphere they bring into your life. Everyone has their downfalls and their imperfections, but those who struggle with G.A.D. cannot take the chance of harbouring an unhealthy relationship.

If someone you care for falls into the category these questions bring to light and they do not bring any sort of substantial positive into your life, then it is time to let them go. This will enable you to build a strong support system, which is vital for someone living and dealing with G.A.D. Human beings are naturally social creatures, and this is why those who struggle with G.A.D. also battle things like bipolar disorders and depression: because sometimes it keeps them from doing what their bodies are naturally programmed to do. Humans are not meant to live in isolation, but G.A.D. can make many people feel that way. If you can build a strong support system, it helps with these feelings of isolation because you have surrounded yourself with individuals who want to lift you up and see you do your best.

Do not ever underestimate the benefit of surrounding yourself with people you know you can truly trust. Not only will they help bring you up during times when you need it the most, they will also be there to talk with you when you feel yourself beginning to spiral. Once you can recognize the symptoms of feeling overwhelmed, you can then tap into this resource of people you have surrounded yourself with who will help coach you through this tough moment in your life.

Then, they can help you talk it out in order to identify the trigger point that began the spiral in the first place. This will help you to establish a list of what to avoid in your life so you are not triggered for these episodes. Every anxiety and worry episode has an origin point that spring boarded your mind into the dark realm of an attack, and sometimes we simply cannot see the trigger point ourselves. Having a supporting network of people to talk to can help identify these points so someone struggling with G.A.D. can better avoid those triggers altogether, therefore reducing the amount of episodes they have.

However, do not jump the gun on diagnosing yourself. Getting yourself to a doctor so they can run certain tests is essential to getting your diagnosis. There are many other things that can cause anxiety and panic problems that are not associated with a G.A.D. diagnosis, and your doctor is going to want to run tests in order to rule those out.

Chapter Two
Now, For Your Check up

In order for your doctor to officially diagnose G.A.D., they will first conduct an overall physical examination. They will look for signs that the anxiety and worry you are experiencing is not linked to any other underlying physical and/or mental condition. They will order blood and urine tests, and probably others if they feel a medical condition is to blame for the anxiety you are experiencing. They will also ask you detailed questions about your medical history as well as your symptoms, so make sure you are as candid with your doctor as you can possibly be. This will help them determine whether this is something that needs to be diagnosed or whether this is something that needs more tests in order to be determined. Then, if necessary, the doctor will utilize a psychological questionnaire in order to help determine a diagnosis.

Many doctors utilize the Diagnostic and Statistical Manual of Mental Disorders in order to help them with an individual's diagnosis. This does not mean they do not know what you are doing, nor does this mean you are "crazy." If your physician relies on this in order to help with a diagnosis, it means they are simply being thorough enough to rule out every other thing that could be causing this before they give you a G.A.D. diagnosis.

Why? Because if an individual is wrongly diagnosed and is given the wrong medication, it can have dire side effects to the quality of life the individual experiences. Not only that, it will help prove to insurance companies of the underlying medical issues going on because of an individual's worries and anxieties, and it will push many insurance companies to cover and/or reimburse for treatments.

But, do not be alarmed if your doctor orders a vitamin deficiency panel regularly if you have already been diagnosed with Generalized Anxiety Disorder, because many vitamins can help abate physical symptoms experienced by those who cope with this disorder on a daily basis.

Once an individual is diagnosed with G.A.D., there is usually some sort of referral to a psychologist or psychiatrist that happens. This is nothing to worry about, but it is precautionary because G.A.D. is usually accompanied by another mental facet that needs to be dealt with. Many people who struggle with G.A.D. also struggle with depression, but some other things that can surface because of G.A.D. are phobias, other panic disorders, PTSD, and feelings of detachment from the world around them that need to be addressed by a mental professional.

Another thing that can cause anxieties and worries of this magnitude to flourish within an individual are vitamin deficiencies. If the human body is deficient in B complex, magnesium, tryptophan, vitamin D, and/or calcium, this can promote feelings of anxiousness and worry because of that those vitamins are inherently impacting when they are not readily available.

For example, if calcium is lacking in the body, the nervous system is going to suffer because calcium is one of the major driving forces behind the balancing of the nervous system. The issue? One of the nervous system's major jobs is to correctly balance chemical impulses within the brain that control emotional states. Some physical symptoms of calcium deficiencies also mimic panic disorders, such as shaking, heart palpitations, and tingling within one's appendages.

Another example: if the body is deficient in vitamin B complexes, the body can begin to experience the slowing down of the nervous system which contributes to exhaustion. This exhaustion, if it spirals, can create fatigue-induced paranoia which feels a great deal like anxiety. However, B complexes are also that vitamin a doctor might recommend for someone who has been diagnosed because studies have shown that this vitamin does effectively help with obsessive impulses.

Magnesium is another one of those vitamins a doctor might recommend an individual take if they are diagnosed with G.A.D. If magnesium is deficient within the body, over 300 biochemical reactions that regulate hormones and stress are affected. But, if taken to help with G.A.D., scientific studies have proven that magnesium can help treat major side effects of depression and anxiety. Magnesium is the most common vitamin deficiency across the world because it is so necessary in thousands of bodily communications and functions throughout the day, yet 75% of individuals across the globe are suffering with its deficiency. Even if your doctor does not recommend an uptick in your magnesium intake, talk to them about it.

Tryptophan, mentioned above, is the number one amino acid that is recommended for purchase in stores when it comes to regulating and helping with stress and anxiety. When this essential amino acid is ingested, it goes through a number of conversion stages before it reaches its final one… which just happens to be serotonin. If you do not know what that is, that is the "feel good" hormone that many people have an imbalance of when experiencing worries, depression, and anxieties. Not only that, but serotonin helps to regulate sleep, moods, and appetites. When deficient, moods are skewed and sleep is hard to come by, and sometimes an appetite can dissipate or even skyrocket. This is one of the first deficiencies physicians look for when running the vitamin panel because it has blaring consequences if not enough of it exists within the body.

Do not be alarmed if your physician asks you to purchase vitamins in order to fill these holes before coming back for another exam. Sometimes being diagnosed with G.A.D. involves simply ruling out all other avenues. They are not trying to shoo you out the door or ignore your issues, they are simply taking your situation one step at a time to make sure their diagnosis is right before sitting down with you and figuring out the path for coping that will be best for your situation.

If the idea of going to the doctor instils a state of panic, then there are some things you can do to prepare for the appointment. You cannot get an official diagnosis without going through a few appointments, but there are things you can formulate yourself that will help you to feel less blindsided by everything going on.

The first is to make lists. Write down the symptoms you experience, the trigger points of your attacks (if identifiable), any health problems you suffer with currently, any medications you are on currently, any family members that deal with similar health issues, and any questions you have for your doctor upfront. This will help to keep your appointment on track and to give your doctor the most valuable and accurate information you can so they can aid you better during this journey.

If you are at a loss for questions to ask, here are some good ones to get you started:

- What tests will I be facing?

- What are the possible things causing my symptoms?

- Are there any printed materials I can take home to read?

- Will medication be necessary? Are there any other avenues than just medication?

- Is a psychologist or psychiatrist going to be necessary?

- Does my family history have anything to do with this?

These types of questions will not only allow you to obtain accurate information according to your case, it will also give the doctor an idea of what is important to you throughout this process. What you ask them is just as important as what you do not ask them, and if you go in unprepared the appointment will be scattered, have no focus, and the doctor might make the assumption that things are not as serious as you proclaim they are.

These lists will help you to stay on top of how you are feeling, what is triggering these feelings, and they will also give your doctor the closest view into your episodes as they will get, which will help them to narrow down prospective diagnoses and causes much easier.

Once your general physician has performed these tests, taken your case step-by-step to rule out other avenues for your anxiety, and evaluated your familial history, then it is time to talk treatment. Unfortunately, many doctors default onto pills and antidepressants in order to help cope with these disorders, and the medications often have dire side effects that dampen one's quality of life even further. Some will recommend an avenue entitled "psychotherapy," where medication is determined by a psychiatrist who sits down with you on a regular basis and talks with you about your life, your current mental state, and your past.

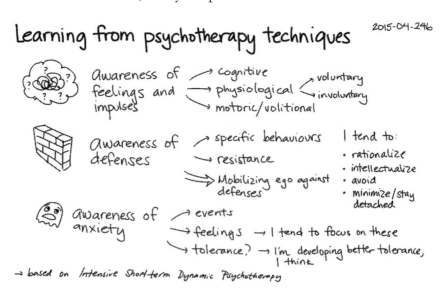

Learning from psychotherapy techniques   2015-04-246

Awareness of feelings and impulses → cognitive → voluntary / involuntary → physiological → motoric/volitional

Awareness of defenses → specific behaviours → resistance ⟹ Mobilizing ego against defenses

I tend to:
- rationalize
- intellectualize
- avoid
- minimize/stay detached

Awareness of anxiety → events → feelings → I tend to focus on these → tolerance? → I'm developing better tolerance, I think

→ based on *Intensive Short-term Dynamic Psychotherapy*

However, anxiety can be personally managed with some easy to follow tips housed in the next chapter. From water intake to going for daily walks, these tips are natural actions that can be controlled by the individual, and sometimes that element of control helps abate symptoms of anxiety and worry in the first place. Keep in mind, there are a host of things an individual can do in order to abate anxiety and dissipate depressive episodes, but the following tips are backed up by scientific studies that have been watched under the close watch of many prominent and intelligent researchers and physicians.

Chapter Three
So, You Have G.A.D.?

Generalized Anxiety Disorder

- 1-year prevalence range from 3 to 8 percent.

- The ratio of women to men with the disorder is about 2 to 1

- 50 to 90 percent of patients with generalized anxiety disorder have another mental disorder

When it comes to managing anxiety, there are two basic ways doctors treat it: psychotherapy and medication. 19 million adults in the United States alone struggle with some sort of diagnosed anxiety disorder, and medications have greatly overshadowed the ability to seek out other forms of help or even implement tactics to that the patient can manage and adjust as necessary on their own. Prescription medications might be the fastest way to treat anxiety disorders, but they come with a multitude of side effects and consequences. Some medications that treat anxiety disorders have some of the highest dependency rates on the market, and sedatives have been known to be the most addictive. Then, some of the side effects that come with antidepressants a physician might prescribe are things such as weight gain, diminished sexual appetites, and upset stomachs.

These are the types of side effects that trigger worrisome states in people with G.A.D. in the first place, so these medications usually end up doing more harm than good in the long run, even though the short term consequences are managing issues pertaining to anxiety disorders. Many research studies have been conducted that show us the fact that pills alone are not substantial enough for a long term treatment for those suffering and coping with anxiety disorders, and should either be combined with psychotherapy, vitamin regimens, and other tactics the patient can implement at home.

Within the world of psychotherapy there are two common forms utilized by experts: cognitive therapy and behavioral therapy. In a cognitive therapy scenario, the therapist helps the particular patient in adapting their triggered thought patterns into ones that are more suitable. For example, the therapist might pinpoint the fact that crowded rooms are a trigger point for the patient, and the therapist will begin to approach the scenario with coping mechanisms the patient can put into practice when thrust into that scenario in order to keep the feeling of panic at bay. But, in behavioral therapy, the therapist helps the patient to battle those undesirable behaviors that rear their heads because of the anxiety. For example, the therapist will guide the patient through relaxation and deep breathing techniques they can utilize whenever the patient begins to experience hyperventilation or shaking as a result of the already panic-induced state.

One of the best things anyone coping with G.A.D. can have is a strong support system. That is why we stressed earlier the importance of getting rid of unhealthy relationships in your life. The people you surround yourself with will always affect how you view the world, how you think about life, and how you feel about yourself. If you are surrounded by people who have positive outlooks on life, it will help to keep your own outlook positive. However, if you are constantly bombarded with individuals who see the downsides to life and disregard the upsides, you will find that it weighs heavier on your shoulders and can even trigger worry-induced episodes more frequently.

However, aside from that, there are other things an individual can do that will help with the long term coping of G.A.D. One of those is to stick to your treatment plan. In the beginning, there will be different things attempted in order to find a combination that works for you. Whenever you do find that golden combination, stick to the treatment plan. Keep your therapy appointments if they are part of your plan, and understand the importance of consistency. When someone is trying to lose weight and they begin a new diet, does the diet work if they only try it for two months and then stop? What happens?

Well, if they have lost any weight at all, they usually gain it back. That is the definition of "yo yo dieting."

Do not "yo yo diet" your anxiety disorder. If it takes you four months to find that golden combination, but you only stick to that combination for a month, when you revert to your old ways you will backtrack in the progress you have made. That is detrimental to your mental health and can prompt harsher panic and anxiety attacks depending on how you are choosing to cope with the scenario.

Another thing that helps many individuals is to join an anxiety support group. In groups like these, just like with any other small group, you can find compassion and understanding for your situation. People will share similar stories that might help ease your mind that you are not alone in your struggles, and it can help you to find people you can confide in that will bring beneficial (and relatable) aspects to your life. If being in a crowd of people is a trigger point for your anxiety, then starting with a small group like this can also be a coping mechanism: you can be social with those who understand you without being surrounded completely with people you do not know.

Something that is incredibly important to this process is the idea of breaking the cycle. The big catch-22 with many people who struggle with anxiety is that they become rooted in their routines, and it this basic routine that incorporates things that trigger their anxiety moments. Therefore, it is imperative you look into ways to break this cycle. If you begin to feel anxious about something, stop and think about what just happened. If it hard to think, go outside and take a walk. Draw in some deep breaths of fresh air. Sometimes simply being cooped up in a room can be anxiety inducing in and of itself. If you do not break the cycle you have fallen into, sometimes you will never be able to identify trigger topics and points you need to stray away from.

Breaking the cycle will help you to better identify those, which will help with your long term coping process with G.A.D.

Another point that many people do not enjoy is the idea of socializing. The biggest trigger point with the 15% of adults who struggle worldwide with anxiety disorders is the idea of socialization. And for many, an experience they have gone through that makes this a trigger is understandable. This is why promotion of small moments of socialization is imperative. For an anxious mind, being cooped up and alone can be detrimental, though the individual might feel as if they are staying away from their trigger point. Some even go as far as to break off ties with best friends and family members. Now, if you have broken off those ties because they were unhealthy, then I congratulate your strength and perseverance. However, if you have broken off those ties because you are avoiding a potential trigger point of socialization, then this is not the best course of action. These loved ones you have cut off can be people you lean on for support and when you need to talk, and isolating yourself from these people can prove even more detrimental.

If socialization is a trigger point, then find ways to avoid high-traffic areas: go to the grocery store either early in the morning or late at night to avoid the crowds; take your lunch break an hour later to avoid the public lunch-hour rush; travel in the middle of the week for your weekend excursion so you are not caught in traffic that might make you anxious; and schedule doctor appointments during low-volume traffic hours. This keeps you around people without being immersed in people, and it can be used as a stepping stone to coping without withdrawing altogether.

However, the most important thing you will ever do is to simply take action. Talk to your doctor instead of merely waiting for them to instruct you. Keep a journal of your feelings, attacks, and trigger points so you can update your doctor accurately. Keep a tally of side effects if you are taking medication so the doctor can adjust as necessary. Find someone who understands and check in with one another. Being proactive about G.A.D. is going to help with long term coping, and can greatly improve the quality of life you will have while still living with an anxiety disorder.

But, these are not the only things you can implement to help you in your journey to cope and manage G.A.D. There are many different things you can do within the comfort of your own home that not only aids in long term management, but are things you can alter yourself in order to find the best balance for you. Keep in mind, your doctor should always know what types of techniques you are implementing, but the following tips will help you to naturally manage your anxiety.

Get The Focus Off Yourself

For example, if you enjoy baking, then utilize that as a coping mechanism for when you begin to feel anxious. If you have a sport you enjoy, then join a team and play. Replacing those anxious thoughts with thoughts and activities of what you love doing will help divert you from a panic-induced scenario.

Aim For Small Victories And Celebrate Them

For example, if you get through your first day without having a panic attack, then celebrate! Have your favorite ice cream flavor or cook yourself your favorite dinner. If you go out and socialize without panicking for the first time, then celebrate it! These little milestones are not only worthy of celebration, the celebration alone can be an encourager when it comes to improving your quality of life.

Indulge In Humorous Activities

Watch a funny movie, or to go a stand-up comedy club. Humor and laughter naturally promote the production of serotonin, which can not only help the body to feel good, but it produces a natural calming sensation.

Eat Healthy Foods

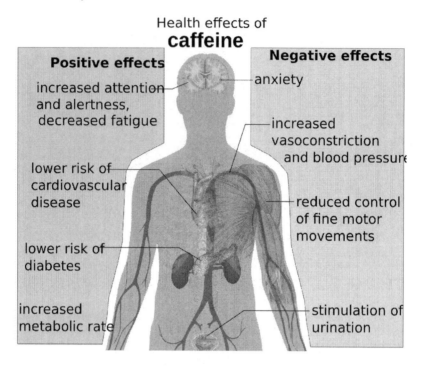

Health effects of
caffeine

Positive effects

increased attention
and alertness,
decreased fatigue

lower risk of
cardiovascular
disease

lower risk of
diabetes

increased
metabolic rate

Negative effects

anxiety

increased
vasoconstriction
and blood pressure

reduced control
of fine motor
movements

stimulation of
urination

There are many foods that are easy to obtain that have been proven to lower anxiety levels. Things like asparagus, oranges, almonds, berries, avocado, salmon, and spinach are all high in things like folic acid and folate, which are two vitamins that are imperative to helping control anxiety. You can find these in any produce section of the grocery store, and they are worth working into your diet on a regular basis in order to help naturally control anxiety and panic.

On the other side, there are certain foods that promote anxious states, such as caffeine, excess amounts of sugar, alcohol, and highly processed meat like hot dogs all have the ability to not only promote anxious and panicked states, but make them worse when they do happen.

Get Out And Lend A Helping Hand

Whether you invest some time indulging in a charity or spend some volunteer time elsewhere, helping those around you who might be unable to help themselves can instill a feeling of purpose, which can naturally alleviate anxious and stressful mindsets.

Get Sleep!

Sleep deprivation can cause a drop in metabolic rates which can result in weight gain, it can destroy the body's immune system, and it can increase one's chances of a cardiac event. Not only that, but the exhaustion that comes with a lack of sleep can produce feelings of paranoia, which trigger anxiety attacks. Getting a good night's sleep not only allows the body necessary time to repair itself from the prior day, it also helps the brain to regulate its own chemical reactions. Get the proper amount of sleep in order to help stave off panic-induced states.

Drink At Least 1.5 Litres Of Water A Day

Water not only helps flush toxins out of the body, it helps to keep the body hydrated. The brain requires a substantial amount of water in order to operate on a daily basis, and if you starve your body of water then you risk inhibiting the balancing of your body's chemical reactions. Not only that, but dehydration can permanently affect other internal organs. If you want your body to be the healthiest it is going to be, then you need to address all facets of your body's health. Keep yourself hydrated in order to help balance chemical and hormonal processes as well as help flush detrimental toxins from your body that are promoting your anxious states.

Dress Confidently

Self-care is one of the biggest components of dealing with anxiousness. Don't take pride in your appearance because society assumes that of you, but take pride in your appearance because it makes you feel better. If you enjoy pedicures, then take yourself to get one! If you love wearing flowing skirts, then go get a couple that look great on you! This can not only serve as a reward mechanism, but it can boost your self-esteem which can help your overall daily attitude.

Take Regular Vacations From Work

Life is innately stressful: we run overtime schedules without overtime pay, and many people are under constant pressure with the fear of losing their job. This is why it is so important to take regular vacations: this time away can help to decompress the mind and get the body out of a situation it has deemed naturally stressful, which can lower the overall chance of an anxiety attack.

Consume Coconut Water, Watermelons, Bananas, And Multivitamins.

Remember when we talked about those vitamins that have been proven to aid those who struggle with anxiety disorders? It is imperative you make sure to work these into your diet. Bananas, in particular, work as a natural beta-blocker, which is a common medication type prescribed by physicians to treat anxiety. Watermelon has one of the highest concentrations of vitamin B6 of any fruit or vegetable on the market, and this vitamin happens to be one that helps aid in the production of brain chemicals that regulate panic and anxiety. Then, there is coconut water, and this liquid is riddled with essential vitamins and minerals that help with not only the regulation of chemicals in the brain that promote anxiety, but also help lower the chance of depression in those who struggle with anxiety-based disorders. Make sure to work all of these things into your diet!

Avoid Uneasy Situations Until You Improve Your Confidence

Use the tactics described above on how to ease yourself back into social situations (i.e.: the examples about staggering your grocery store visits). If you have particular phobias, then you have the option of seeking out immersive treatment in order to help combat those phobias, should you wish.

Have Someone You Can Talk To

Always have a close friend or family member you can talk to about issues you are struggling with. Knowing you are not the only one to shoulder them can really ease the mind's overall disposition.

Take Regular Walks

Take a 10-minute walk everyday to take in the sights, smells, and sounds. This not only works as a wonderful distraction tactic, but it also helps to slowly re-immerse yourself into the world gradually if you have withdrawn heavily from it due to your anxiety disorder.

Meditate To Find Inner Peace

Meditate 10-15 minutes a day. This can clear vital mental blockages and help you become more in tune and aware with your inward disposition, which can help alleviate self-induced anxiety clouds.

Find A New Job!

If part of your anxiety and unhappiness is caused by your job, then begin to look for a new one. Put your resume out on websites like Indeed and Monster.com and open yourself up to what else might be out there. Sometimes a change in an individual's career path can alleviate a great deal of stress. If no doors are open to you, then going back to school is always an option.

Watch Positive Psychological Videos

YouTube channels such as GoalCast, MotivationGrid, Ben Lionel Scott frequently post incredible motivational videos geared towards inspiring the mind to do what it feels it cannot. Watching these types of videos are a great way to personally lift your disposition without taxing your brain with reading mindless text copy.

Surround Yourself With Positive People

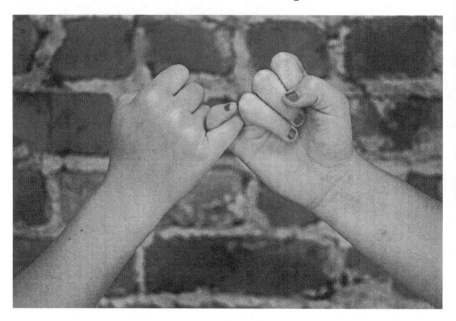

The people you surround yourself with will always affect you in some way. If you keep positive individuals around you, then they will affect you in positive ways.

If you follow all of these things outlined above, then you will be well on your way to properly managing your anxiety on your own. Contrary to popular belief, anxiety is manageable and, in some cases, completely curable. This is why it is imperative to make sure these tips are followed to the best of your ability: the more you can do on your own, the less dependency you will have on outside forces to help you cope. This will not only help you boost your self-esteem, but it will increase your own confidence in yourself to be able to live your life they way you see fit.

The one thing you have to understand, throughout this entire journey, is that G.A.D. is not a prison.

Chapter Four
G.A.D. Is Not A Prison

What you have to understand is that you are not alone. Anxiety disorders affect 19% of adults in the United States alone, which comes to around 40 million adults between the ages of 18 and 54. But, the scariest statistic is that a theorized 30% of adults around the world struggle with undiagnosed anxiety issues. These adults are not seeking treatment, are not attempting coping techniques, and are not under the care of a careful doctor helping them navigate this scary journey they are on. But, out of the 19% of adults that do seek treatment, only 10% of them will actually be treated correctly.

This is why it is important to keep a journal of your symptoms and trigger points and always ask questions. We trust our physicians to always look out for our best interest, but they can only work with the information we give them.

One of the biggest factors many doctors and psychologists look at is whether an individual is happy at their job. Why? Because a whopping 41% of adults worldwide proclaim that the bulk of their anxiety comes from their workplace. Not being happy with one's career path only makes that toll taken upon the body worse.

Anxiety disorders, and especially G.A.D., are the most common types of mental illness in the United States. They are highly treatable and very manageable, and those that stay on top of their treatments and seek regular help from physicians who can help them go on to lead a high quality of life. Unfortunately, only 30% of those who do struggle with panic-and-anxiety-induced disorders actually reach out for treatment.

Not only that, but close to 50% of those who are diagnosed with an anxiety disorder are also clinically diagnosed with depression. It is very common for the two to go hand-in-hand, which is why so many medicinal treatments have gotten out of hand. The tips listed above are ways any individual can properly manage their anxiety and worried states in a healthy way that does not risk the possibility of addiction to medication or the reception of improper treatment tactics. You should always seek out a physician's help and inform them of the things you are trying, but if your physician does not support the routes you wish to try, then do not be afraid to reach out for a second opinion.

After all, this is your life. Taking control of your medical treatments will better enable you to find long term ways of coping with G.A.D., as well as any other diagnoses that might follow as a result of your struggles with anxiety and panic. But, it prompts a reiteration of two very specific facts: 1) you are not alone, and 2) anxiety is manageable. It is possible to live a wonderful, social, fulfilling life after being diagnosed with an anxiety disorder, and if all the trigger points are addressed and dealt with, it is possible to be rid of the anxiety disorder altogether.

These statistics are staggering, considering the number of people living with an undiagnosed anxiety disorder. As technology evolves and distracting sounds become an everyday part of our lives, our focus always seems to be ripped from one task to another at the drop of a specific sound. Not only that, but with the connection technology allows, it also produces "workaholics" that end up taking the bulk of their work home, meaning all of that in-office stress makes its way into their houses. The mind is a powerful mechanism, with a clock speed of 200 firings per second. That means the average human brain kickstarts processes that enable us to interpret and retain information 200 separate times per second.

That amounts to over 17 million kickstarts a day.

This means the brain can create associations between the physical world and our emotional world incredibly quickly. People who bring their work home with them, and all the stresses that come with that work, will soon find themselves anxious in their own homes and beds even if they have relieved themselves of work for the day. Why? Because their brain has used a few of those 17 million computations to reinforce that stress and negative emotion with a physical object you routinely sit and or on. This can become very dangerous for people who struggle with anxiety disorders, and it is another reason the rate of adults who do diagnosably struggle with G.A.D. is steadily climbing.

Even though technology has made our lives easier, it has also made our lives more stressful, which has opened the door for more anxiousness.

We admit, there has been a lot of information thrown at you in this book. So, below is a printable page that houses a summarization of everything we have given you. Anyone can print out and tack it onto their bathroom mirror, slip it into their work bag, or even tape it to their refrigerator so they can keep reminding themselves of things they need to do. From what you need for every appointment to tactics you can utilize to help keep your anxiety at bay, these bullet points will help you in your journey to healthily cope with your anxiety and, hopefully, eliminate it altogether.

If you have read through this book, I am proud of you. Just reading this material means you have acknowledged that something is not right and are searching for answers to questions you have. Taking these first steps ensures that you are well on your way to a full recovery, and that takes a great deal of courage and strength.

However, there are many people with anxious thoughts and feelings right now about purchasing this guide. Many people who suffer with anxiety and panic talk themselves out of things that can be beneficial for them because of the uncertainty behind it all. Please, if this guide has helped you in any way, leave a review of this book. Tell those who are still struggling how it helped you and encourage them to seek the knowledge and education within the walls of this guide. Help them to make the same brave, life-changing choice you have.

Both myself and the person your testimony helps will be forever grateful for your review.

Quick Anxiety Relief Guide

Print out this page and keep it somewhere you can easily spot. This summarization list will help you with everything from what you need to take with you to every medical appointment all the way down to outlining the tips you can implement on your own to help manage your anxiety within your own home.

For your medical appointments, always have:

- Your updated journal with trigger points and symptoms.

- Any questions you want to ask your doctor.

Adopt these tips for in-home care of your anxiety episodes:

- Focus on yourself and not on your thoughts.

- Celebrate every single small victory.

- Always indulge in activities filled with humor.

- Keep a healthy diet.

- Make sure to work multivitamins, bananas, watermelons, and coconut water into your diet as well.

- Drink at least a half a gallon of water every day.

- Volunteer your time at homeless shelters or care centers to help get out and be of service to someone else.

- Get ample amounts of rest at night.

- Don't be afraid to invest in yourself and dress nicely!

- Take regular vacations and breaks from work in order to do something you love to do without the pressures from work weighing on you.

- Do not intentionally place yourself in uneasy situations before you are ready; rather, ease into them slowly.

- Have a close friend or family member you can talk to about your problems and worries without being judged.

- Take a 10-minute walk daily while taking big, deep breaths of fresh air.

- Meditate 10-15 minutes every single day in a space where you feel comfortable and at ease in.

- If your job is producing the most anxiety, then take the steps necessary to look into other job opportunities.

- Watch one positive psychology video everyday in order to help relieve your mind of your anxious trains of thought and replace them with something to think about.

- Keep the company of positive and happy people.

Printed in Great Britain
by Amazon

37676144R00031